DYNAMIC
KICKING
METHOD

Disclaimer

DYNAMIC KICKING METHOD

◇◇ MASAFUMI SHIOMITSU ◇◇

Published by

dragon books

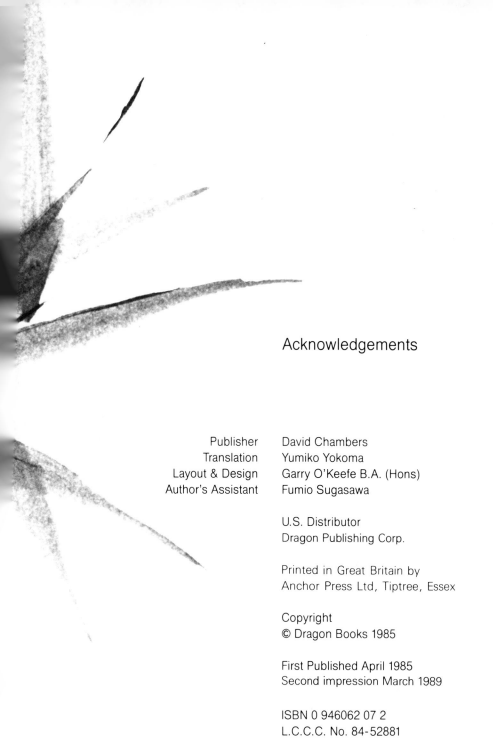

Acknowledgements

Publisher	David Chambers
Translation	Yumiko Yokoma
Layout & Design	Garry O'Keefe B.A. (Hons)
Author's Assistant	Fumio Sugasawa

U.S. Distributor
Dragon Publishing Corp.

Printed in Great Britain by
Anchor Press Ltd, Tiptree, Essex

First Published April 1985
Second impression March 1989

ISBN 0 946062 07 2
L.C.C.C. No. 84-52881

Contents

和道流空手道連盟総本部

I take pleasure in recommending this book by Masafumi Shiomitsu who is a long time member of the Wado-Ryu, and one of its leading pioneers in the United Kingdom.

As everybody knows, when he was a student at Nihon University, he was famous for his kicking ability, and was regarded by all as the very best in the school at that period. It is clear that time has added to, rather than diminished his ability in this area.

Karate kicking techniques are extremely powerful, when mastered: several times more powerful than striking techniques for example. However they must be learnt thoroughly, otherwise they tend to be weak and ineffective, and on occasions, hazardous to the performer.

The author is to be complimented on the clarity of the photographs, and comprehensive nature of the text, which when combined, should allow the student to correctly learn these fascinating techniques, and with practice, go on to master them.

It is my opinion, that this book by Masafumi Shiomitsu, is a valuable contribution to the art of Karate-do, and one for which he should be commended.

大塚博紀

Hironori Ohtsuka
Principal of the World Wado Ryu.

In this small book I have tried to show that the number of weapons in the arsenal of karate kicks, is only limited to the skill, determination and imagination of the performer.

It is commonly thought, largely as a result of the influence of Karate competition for example, that Mae-Geri is always performed using the ball of the foot to attack the stomach or chest, and similarly, that Mawashi-Geri roundhouse kick is always directed at the opponent's head, also using the ball of the foot.

Nothing could be further from the truth, and yet when these two techniques are mentioned, these applications immediately spring to most people's minds. In fact, as I have tried to show, depending upon the circumstances, Mae-Geri can be performed using the heel, toes or instep, as can Mawashi-Geri. Therefore, in the interest of clarity I have described the techniques in this book, firstly by their most commonly known name, and therefore application, (for example, Kakato-Geri as a downward kick with the heel), then described some, but not all of the many variations, by means of applications, each of which in their own way, are techniques in themselves.

In this way I hope to help students both understand the techniques better, develop greater all round kicking ability and to learn to be flexible, which is one of the secrets of success in Karate-Do. The other secret, if that is the correct description, is hard and relentless effort. When you train, alone or in the dojo, do so with maximum effort and concentration, put your full power into every punch or kick, and by doing so learn to overcome your own weakness, fatigue, boredom and lack of spirit. Achieve this, and providing your attitude is a serious one, you will make good progress. Remember that every drop of sweat you shed when training is worth more than the black belt you may be wearing.

The study of Karate-Do is the work of a lifetime. As you practice you will learn new skills, and polish old ones, and by doing so become a better person both physically and mentally. If, through this small book I have helped even one student closer to this goal, I will consider my efforts in writing this book well rewarded.

1940 Born November 24th in Kagoshima Prefecture, Japan.

1955 Began study of the Shorin Ryu style of Karate with a local teacher.

1959 Entered Nihon University and became a member of the Wado Ryu style Karate club.

1962 Leader of team that won the 'Zen Nihon Wado Ryu' championships, (All Japan Wado Ryu style match).

1963 Officially appointed as captain of Nihon University Karate Team.

1964 Graduated from university with a degree in ecomonics. Graded 4th dan in Wado Ryu Karate.

1965 Appointed assistant Chief Instructor to Britain.

1969 Instructor to Spain and France.

1972 Appointed as instructor to Madagascar.

1976 Returned to original position in Britain.

1981 Returned to Japan to celebrate the 90th birthday of the founder of Wado Ryu Karate, and awarded 7th Dan by him.

1983 Official Instructor to European Wado Ryu Karate organisations, Vice President of European Wado Kai.

Master Shiomitsu was one of the first instructors of Japanese Karate-Do, to take the message of this unique combatitive art to the then, largely ignorant outside world. Back in the sixties, the powerful and dramatic demonstrations by him and his contemporaries inspired many thousands of non-Japanese to take up the study of this ancient oriental method of self defence, and from the ranks of these pioneers, come the Karate champions of this present generation.

Son of a successful publisher and product of a fine university education, his sophistication, intelligence and knowledge of English, do not in any way conform to the modern image of an oriental Karate Master. Yet, in the competition arena and the Dojo, he was and is, respected if not feared. His Mawashi-Geri and Mae-Geri are devastating, and it is said, have never been seen by those who have fallen victim to them. Affable, well-mannered and even tempered, he is nonetheless a tough and dedicated Karate man, and it must have been with great relief, that his peers witnessed his departure from Japan in 1965, to take up the position of assistant to Tatsuo Suzuki 8th Dan Hanshi, Chief Instructor to Europe for the All Japan Wado Kai.

While he is without doubt one of the finest and most effective 'kickers' of the post war period, a man who can unleash devastating kicks with the precision of a surgeon wielding a scalpel, he does so with what many commentators on modern Karate would regard as a handicap, namely a powerful, heavily built physique. So used were we to seeing slightly built instructors, dazzling audiences with flying reverse Mawashi-Geri roundhouse kicks and the like, that even those who should have known better eventually equated kicking ability with wiryness and lack of muscle. However, deep down inside many of us there were nagging doubts about the effectiveness of these exotic techniques, and the ability of the performers to deliver them on target, at the right time and with sufficient force to knock the opponent down.

The techniques looked good, the students liked them, and they often persuaded competition judges, in the event of a draw, to give the benefit of the doubt to the competitor who had attempted a 'crowd pleaser' rather than to his opponent who had performed a more mundane technique, even though the latter might have been widely recognised as being far more effective, and therefore more likely to have finished the match in a real contest of skills. Competition Karate grew in following and influence year by year, until eventually the techniques used became so geared to competition, that doubts about their effectiveness in self defence situations were raised, and slowly but inevitably, the pendulum began to swing back to the traditional techniques that were developed from, and tempered by, the actual combat situations experienced by the Karate masters of Okinawa and Japan in a previous age.

During his career as a top flight competitor and internationally known instructor, Masafumi Shiomitsu has always adhered to the traditional teachings and training methods for the most practical reasons; their ability to weld together technique, power and perfect timing and by doing so, create kicks that penetrate the most powerful and stubborn defence. Flexible to the extent that he believes all techniques must be performed creatively, and not 'by numbers', he maintains that his undeniable power and ability are the result of these traditional methods, and that this is a part of a student's education which must not be neglected if success is to be achieved.

The kicking techniques that he demonstrates in this book are both practical, for self defence application, and in most cases, suitable for competition. Many purists may be surprised by the directness and power of the movements shown, let me remind them that this is how things were, when Karate was first developed for the unarmed defence of the person in the most effective way possible, and when no consideration was given to the aesthetic appearance of a technique, or to its value for points scoring.

Regretably, no book however well photographed or designed, can completely convey to the reader the power and effectiveness of a Karate technique, at the instant that it is performed by such a talented and experienced teacher. Only by witnessing it at first hand can the combination of speed, accuracy and explosive power be appreciated. All we can do is to assure the reader that we have done our very best to lay before you in this volume the ability, theories and experience of this unique instructor so that you can benefit from his knowledge, and by doing so, improve your own performance of the art of Karate-Do.

Equally at home in the West, as in his native Japan, Master Shiomitsu is the modern product of a traditional school of hard Karate, the object of which, then as now, is the development of power and technique, sufficient to deter or defeat any aggressor, and through this, the formation of good character, wisdom and experience of life, that will allow the possessor of this valuable knowledge, to use his talents to the advantage of society in general.

Practicing Pinan Shodan Kata, 1965.

The Way of Karate-Do and the Importance of Etiquette

In Karate-Do, as with all traditional Japanese martial arts, exercise and training begin with and are concluded by, a formal bow, either standing or sitting depending on the circumstances. This is probably the most visible sign of the system of etiquette known in Japan as REIGI that is fundamental both to the fighting systems, and the people of the Japanese archipelago, and yet is almost always misunderstood even by quite experienced, and physically capable students of the martial arts.

As with all complex activities involving the simultaneous use of mind and body, no verbal or written explanation will adequately explain what the student should be feeling within himself, when he performs any particular movement or exercise. Only experience and hard training will make him aware of that, but as a guide and as a series of ideas and concepts to consider, I offer the reader the following explanation of the importance of etiquette, as manifested by the traditional bow, and the reasons for which it is performed.

When you bow, you not only show respect for your opponent and the training hall, but by gathering and controlling your inner power and remaining calm and dignified in your manner, you emanate an aura of quiet confidence and invulnerability that will allow you to influence those around you, and exercise a degree of control over them. By understanding this, and developing it as an essential, and not just a superficial part of your training programme, the bow will become almost like a formal Karate stance or Kamae, in which you quickly take control of any situation you face, while remaining ready to defend yourself without the need to be constantly tense.

This may seem to be no more than a ploy to unsettle an opponent in order to make him easier to defeat, an attempt to upset his concentration and exert psychological pressure in order to gain an easy victory. While this does happen in modern sports, and has become almost a tradition in some, it is not true in the case of the martial arts, as there was, and often is, too much at stake to risk the outcome of physical combat on a trick. In fact we all have the instinctive ability, together with most other members of the animal kingdom, to recognise the leader of any group, whether we are a member of that group or not. He may not be the oldest, or the most experienced, but all recognise him as the leader, and defer to him. Some people are born with this power, others have to acquire it; the serious study of Karate-Do is an excellent way of developing this ability, and at the same time building a strong healthy body and learning to defend yourself.

When your prepare to bow, this is the sort of force you must exert, a combination of confidence, strength of character, dignity and awareness. If you can do this successfully you will possess a powerful weapon, as your calmness will be communicated to those around you through your body language, and they will understand your latent strength and invulnerability. It was by the use of this force, and not through threats or violence or naked aggression, that the Samurai of Japan's past ages controlled large groups of people, keeping order when disorder was threatened, and arresting wrongdoers without even drawing their swords.

This power or ability must never by confused with aggression, which in my opinion is a negative emotion caused by fear, and is therefore counter-productive. It is also a sign of weakness, in that your opponent has instilled fear in you and you have reacted by becoming aggressive, he therefore gains a superior position, having discovered that he can exercise a degree of control over you. A dog that is frightened will growl and threaten, his hair will stand up, and he will present a fearsome appearance to his enemy. The courageous dog, will attack without warning, fear is unknown to him and he wisely does not want to lose the element of surprise.

Powerful positive action should never be mistaken for aggression, and aggression should never be taken for strength, when you understand this and have experienced it, you will realise the importance of etiquette, and why it's observance is insisted upon by all good instructors.

Receiving the trophy from Boh Sensei, former President of the Wado Federation, as captain of the winners of the team event at the All Japan Championships in 1962.

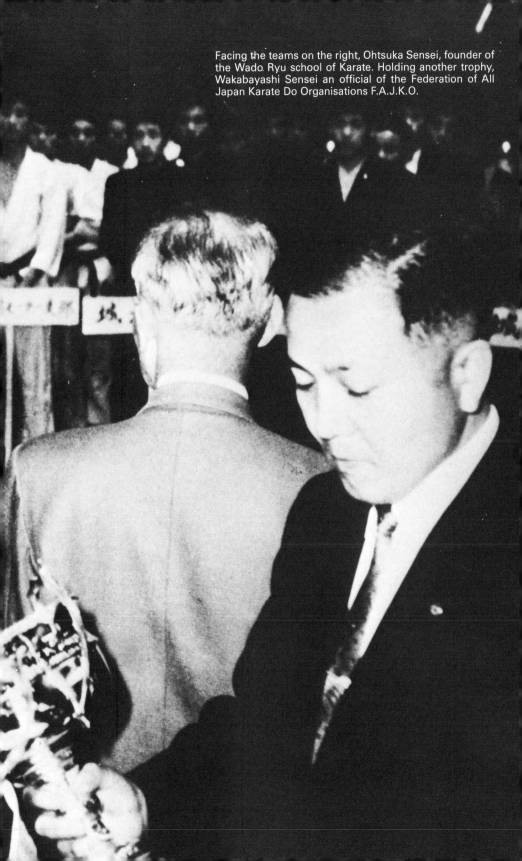

Facing the teams on the right, Ohtsuka Sensei, founder of the Wado Ryu school of Karate. Holding another trophy, Wakabayashi Sensei an official of the Federation of All Japan Karate Do Organisations F.A.J.K.O.

Tachi Rei
The Standing Bow

1. Stand upright in a relaxed manner with the hands by the side and back straight, but not unnaturally so like a soldier.

2. The feet should be at a slight angle to each other in the Musubi-dachi stance.

3. Look into your opponent's eyes, without staring, then bow from the waist taking care not to duck the head too far forward.

4. Pause slightly, then return to the relaxed upright position.

Za Rei The Seated Bow

1. Stand upright with the shoulders relaxed and the feet slightly apart in the Musubi-dachi stance.

2. Twist your body towards the left so that your right knee points towards your opponent and placing your hands slowly on the front of your thighs, bend your knees...

Guide to Bowing

The method in which the standing and sitting bows are performed may vary slightly from school to school, and in the performance of the mechanical action of bowing, nobody can claim to know the only correct way, as there are so many 'correct' methods, depending on who your instructor was, and what style of Karate you have studied. I was taught in the following fashion, and I offer it therefore as a guide to students who have not already grown into a particular method or tradition.

3. ...so that your right touches the floor first, followed by the left.

Za Rei The Seated Bow

4. Straighten your toes, and with your insteps flat on the floor, sit into the hollow made by your heels, keeping the knees tense and partially supporting the body still so that a minute gap, the thickness of a piece of paper, can be maintained between your heels and your seat. While sitting prior to the actual bow, remain calm and dignified, do not move the body around unnecessarily or fidget. Show respect to your opponent and be ready to defend yourself against an attack from any direction.

6. Watching your opponent carefully, slide the hands forward and down so that they describe a curved path down the outside of your legs...

7. ...and place them on the floor in front of you, with the hands formed into the shape of a triangle, the index fingers and thumbs touching.

Za Rei The Seated Bow

8. Bow slightly from the waist, avoiding at all costs showing the top of your head, or nape of your neck to the opponent, and return to the upright seated position.

To return to the standing position, slide the left leg forward to take the weight of the body, turn the toes of the right foot under, then continuing to rise, slide the right foot forward into the original Musubi-Dachi stance. This movement must be performed slowly and smoothly, your eyes never leaving your opponent for an instant.

5. Side view.

As there are many ways of bowing, so there are also many ways of breathing during the performance of a bow, each instructor having his own preferred method, which he will pass onto his students. All are agreed that breathing must be calm and deep, performed from the lower abdomen, and that exhalation must be slow and complete. A frequency of five or six breaths per minute should be maintained as in the study of Za Zen seated meditation. Until you practice breathing like this while seated in the correct Zen position, you will never realise just how calm and relaxed you can be.

As a general rule, inhale when seated prior to the actual bow, then exhale as you incline your body forward. As you complete the bow, aim to have about 80% of the air left in your lungs. Continue exhaling until you resume the upright seated position, then inhale again using the lower stomach as the starting point of the beathing cycle.

Breathing during sparring must of necessity be light and short, and it is important that you do not let your opponent observe your method for breathing, or he could defeat you by manipulating your rhythm to his own advantage.

The Dojo or Training Hall

The Dojo (Do-way, method or path, Jo-a place) was named after the area used by Buddhist monks for prayer and meditation, and represents therefore not only the place to learn the techniques of a particular martial art, but also a place for the education of the soul. It is not just a hall where students practice sparring or perform Kata, but a school of life where, through his triumphs and failures, joy and despair, the student of Karate-Do becomes a whole person, and learns to live the life he has been given, correctly, and to the advantage of himself and society.

The tradition of physical and spiritual conditioning, combined with serious academic or artistic study, has long been a feature of the martial arts of Japan, and can still be recommended to today's student. Miyamoto Musashi, Japan's greatest ever swordsman, a ferocious fighter who was undefeated when he died of old age, was an accomplished author and painter, proving that a strong mind and a trained body are an unbeatable combination.

Whether it be a jewel of medieval Japanese architecture, or the humblest training hall or gymnasium, respect the Dojo of which you are a member. When you enter its doors, commit yourself to maximum effort, treat all who train there with respect, act with humility, and you will learn things that will benefit you through your entire life.

As the techniques of Karate involve the use of every part of the body, it is essential in order to avoid unnecessary injury, that you exercise and stretch your muscles before and after training. It is equally important that this is done slowly and systematically so that the primary sets of muscles are gradually stretched, and that while performing the exercises shown in this book, your breathing be regular and comfortable.

Therefore, when you perform an exercise, slowly extend your movements until you feel that you are stretched to the limit, then holding the position, breath slowly and deeply for ten to twenty seconds, before relaxing. Perform the same movement again, three or four times, relaxing between each performance. This is particularly important if you wish to make kicking your speciality, as these powerful techniques can easily cause discomfort and actual injury, if your preparation is inadequate.

Just as important is to finish your training session with exercises that will relax the body, make joints supple and return your muscles to their original state.

Time spent exercising is never wasted, warming and conditioning the body before training, and exercising to relax afterwards is vital if you wish to perform well, improve your technique and enjoy tough work-outs free from injury and discomfort.

Important.

If at any time during training you feel that an injury has occured, stop immediately and if the pain persists, seek professional help.

*Denotes a change in exercise position

*Starting position.

Bend at the knees, keeping the back straight. Hold for 10-20 seconds and repeat.

Breathing normally, bend to touch the floor without ducking your head, and repeat.

*Crouch down over one foot, gradually stretching the opposite knee as much as possible. Hold for 10-20 seconds and perform on both sides.

Stand with the feet spread as far apart as possible.

Lower your body into the position shown. Hold and repeat.

Assume this deep stance on both sides, attempting to keep the heel of the leading foot flat on the floor. Hold and repeat.

Keeping the foot of the leading leg flat on the floor, push the point of the elbow as low as possible.

Face the front, then slowly lower the body as far as possible while breathing as normally as possible. Hold and repeat.

Holding the position, lean your body to the left and hold your ankle for 20 seconds. Return to the upright position keeping your back straight and repeat another 2 times. Same for right hand side.

*Assume the position shown, then lean forward as far as possible while facing to the front.

Breathing normally, reach forward to grasp your toes. Hold and repeat.

Gradually spread your legs as wide as possible...

...then breathing as normally as you are able, bend forward as far as you can. Try to put your elbows flat on the floor.

Tuck one leg up close to your body, then lean forward as far as possible, keeping the opposite leg straight with the toes pointing upwards.

Retaining the same basic position as before, bend from the waist to touch the toes. Hold and repeat both sides.

Support yourself with one arm behind, then using the supporting arm, raise yourself, at the same time bringing the opposite arm up and over to stretch the body. Perform on both sides.

Stretch along the length of each leg to grasp your toes. Hold, then perform on the other side.

Place your hand on the leg tucked into the body, then stretch across to touch the toes of the opposite leg. Breathe as naturally as possible. Hold and repeat.

These last three exercises link up very well and should flow naturally into each other.

*Sitting upright, place the soles of the feet together and press the knees down towards the floor.

Drawing your feet towards you, bend forward and hold the position.

...then in a continuous movement, twist your leg to the side and pull up to the head while keeping the head upright as shown. Hold 10-20 seconds, repeat on both sides.

*With one leg under your body, stretch the other as much as possible by pushing the heel forward...

*Gradually lower your body onto your legs with the feet pointing outwards.

*Pull your leg towards you and hold the knee as close to the body as possible...

...then from the same position, gradually lower your body to the floor. Hold and repeat both sides.

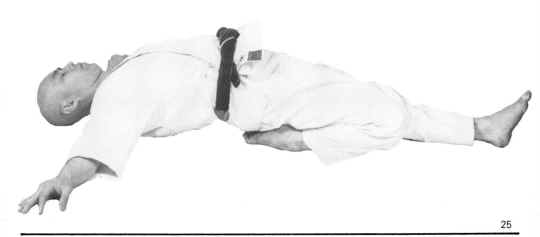

Tuck both legs under...

...then lean backwards as far as possible, keeping as much of your shins in contact with the floor as you can.

...then after holding for 10-20 seconds, roll backwards, keeping the legs absolutely straight.

*With one leg crossed over the other, push against your knee and twist around as far as possible. Repeat on both sides.

*Pull your knees up to your chest and grasp your toes.

Keeping hold of your toes, stretch both legs while balancing on the lowest part of your back...

Lay on your back, then pull your knee as high and as close to your chest as you can. Repeat on both sides.

Holding the toes, stretch each leg in turn, and hold for 10-20 seconds.

*Lie on your side, then grasping the upper leg, push against the restraining hand as hard as possible.

Keeping the same position, stretch the knees by putting pressure on the legs in an upward direction. Repeat both sides.

...finally, holding down your knee, twist your body round as far as possible in the opposite direction.

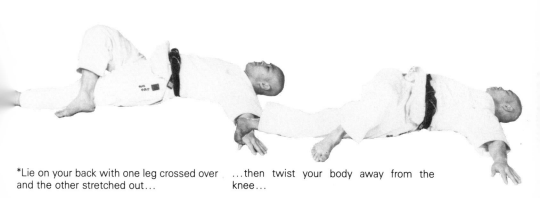

*Lie on your back with one leg crossed over and the other stretched out...

...then twist your body away from the knee...

Important

Do not expect overnight results, the instructor demonstrating these exercises, has only achieved this degree of flexibility through repeated practice over a long period. Always exercise before and after training, and remember that injuries caused as a result of not stretching and conditioning the body, and the practice time lost as a result of them, is a major reason for slow progress in Karate.

Push against your partner as hard as you can by straightening your back leg and driving hard against the floor with your heel.

With your partner holding your foot in a heel up, toes down position, stretch forward as far as possible. Hold and repeat.

With your ankles touching your partner's, slowly pull his arms to stretch his knees.

With your legs in a 'splits' position, your partner slowly raises your leading leg.

Crouch down, then slowly rise to your full height, to stretch your partner's leg. Hold and repeat both sides.

Holding your partner's ankles, pull slowly towards you to stretch his knees and spine.

Both partners put their knees together and grasp hands...

...then with their spines held straight, both gradually lower themselves as far as possible.

Both partners put the soles of their feet together, so that the outside edges touch the floor, then staying as relaxed as possible...

...they lower themselves as far as they can.

Making sure your partner keeps his back straight...

...help him to lean forward as far as possible, while he breathes as normally as he can.

As your partner holds his toes, help him to lean forward as far as possible.

As you push him, he pulls his toes towards himself, thus stretching his Achilles tendons.

Rock your partner gently sideways as far as possible, as he sits with his legs spread wide, knees straight, and toes turned upwards.

Help your partner bend from the waist as far as possible, over each of his legs in turn.

As your partner holds the soles of his feet together, gently press his knees down to the floor.

To prevent your partner's knees leaving the floor as you push him backwards, hold them down with your own knees, while pressing on his hips with his legs bent under him.

With is feet tucked in close to his groin, push your partner forward from the waist, to bring his chest over his feet. Make sure that he keeps his knees flat on the floor.

As your partner lays on the floor bend his knee inwards, push down on his knee, and on the opposite side of his pelvis.

Holding one of your partner's legs down with your knee, slowly stretch the other one upwards. Repeat both sides.

With your partner holding the soles of his feet together, gradually force his knees apart as far as possible.

To stretch further, hold down one leg by placing your foot on the ankle, then slowly raise the other, making sure that the knee stays straight.

Holding your partner's toes, push his legs down as far as possible. Partner should exert maximum resistance against the downward pressure.

Warming Down 1   **Warming Down 2**

With your partner lying face down, immobilise his leg with your foot, and holding his leg below the ankle, pull as hard as possible to relieve the knee cartilage...

...then bend his leg down as far as it will go.

Holding your partner's ankle, bend his leg as far as possible...

...then pull down strongly <u>along</u> the floor five or six times on either side.

Warming Down 5

(Both pictures)

Warming Down 3   **Warming Down 4**

Straighten up so as to stretch your partner   Pull your partner's legs upwards by
backwards.   straightening your own back.

Partner lies on the floor in a relaxed state as   With your partner lying relaxed on his back,
you bend his legs fully to exercise the hip   pull strongly on his ankles.
joint.

Warming Down 6

(Both pictures)

Warming Down 7   **Warming Down 8**

Holding your partner's shoulders down with your hand and knee, push his knee across his body as far as possible. Repeat on both sides.

Finally, straighten your partner's back by suspending him from your neck.

This chapter contains all the exercises that you should ever need to prepare muscles for training, and relax them afterwards. As stated previously, suitable exercises should be performed before and after training without fail. Techniques such as Mawashi-Geri and Kakato-Geri place great strain on the back, so unless you are fully warmed up before performing them, you may eventually experience some lower back pain or discomfort.

Choose the exercises that suit you best from this section, and do not neglect to perform them.

Please Note

Though all the exercises shown may be used for warming down, the eight I have specified must always be performed when warming down, as they are beneficial to the spine, groin and knee joints.

THE LEGS AS WEAPONS

The Legs as Weapons

So that the total power of a kicking technique can be focused and delivered to the target with maximum efficiency, the contact point, usually part of the foot, must be formed into a 'weapon'. These are the most common 'weapons' used in conjunction with Karate kicking techniques.

The toes are bunched together for use with front kicks.

The ball of the foot is used with Mae-Geri front kick, and Mawashi-Geri roundhouse kick.

Front view

The instep can also be used with Mawashi-geri.

The knee is one of the body's most powerful weapons.

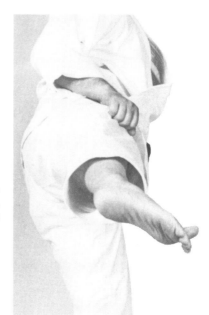

The side kick employs the outside edge of the foot to strike the target, and is known as Sokuto, literally leg sword. This technique can also be used as a block.

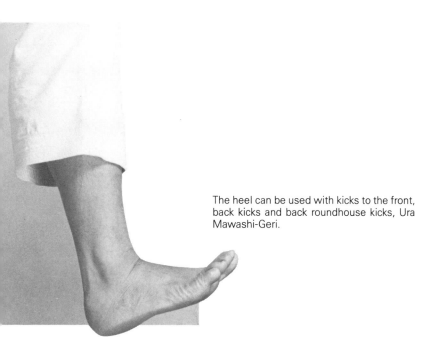

The heel can be used with kicks to the front, back kicks and back roundhouse kicks, Ura Mawashi-Geri.

To strengthen your toes and ankles for kicking, practice walking in the ways shown here. Exercise 1 is for the more advanced student, while exercises 2 and 3 should be practised by beginners.

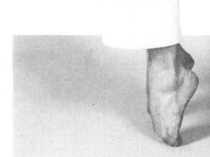

Exercise 1. Advanced level.

Exercise 2. Beginner.   Exercise 3. Beginner.

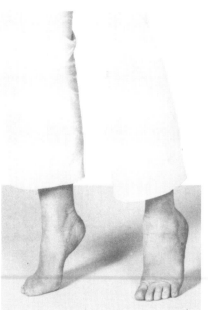

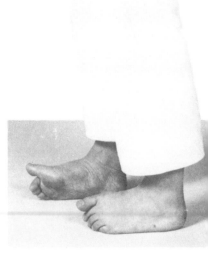

The nerve points shown on the two charts reproduced overleaf, are those used in the art of Atemi-waza, and represent the most vulnerable points of the human body, and therefore the most effective targets for kicks or punches.

Points that are shown on the centre line are single targets, while those occuring away from the centre line, occur in pairs, either side of and equidistant from the centre line.

To avoid confusion, those nerve points that occur on the hands and arms have been omitted.

Depending on the school of karate, different names exist for all these points. Those that I have listed belong to the style that I practice but by way of an example, the point on the top of the head that I have called Ten Dou is known in other schools as, Ten To, Hyaku E, San Jo, Jo Ton and Ten Jo.

Needless to say, because of the damage that can be done by striking these vulnerable nerve points, great care must be exercised, and it is for this reason that only the most senior, capable and responsible students are ever introduced to this advanced level of study.

Important Notice

Unless you have studied for some time under a qualified teacher, and practised a great deal it will be difficult if not impossible to find these points successfully, however, **you should never, even in fun, attempt to strike someone on one of these vulnerable points.** They are included in this book as reference material **only**.

TEN DOU

LEFT RYO MOU

RIGHT KASUMI

UTC

JIMON

NICHI GETSU

DOKKO

BI SEN

RIGHT MURASAME

JIN CHU

LEFT MATSUKAZE

KA KON

JINGEI

HI CHU

UNGETSU

GAN CHU

DAN CHU

GAN KA

KYOUSEN

DEN KOU

SUIGETSU

LEFT TSUKIKAGE

RIGHT INAZUMA

MYOJO

KIKA

HOKUSHIN

TSURIGANE

FŪSHI

KEKKA

SEN RYU

SARABON

FUKUTO

ASHI SANRI

SOTO KURUBUSHI

SAN IN KO

RINKYU

UCHI KURUBUSH

TAI CHU

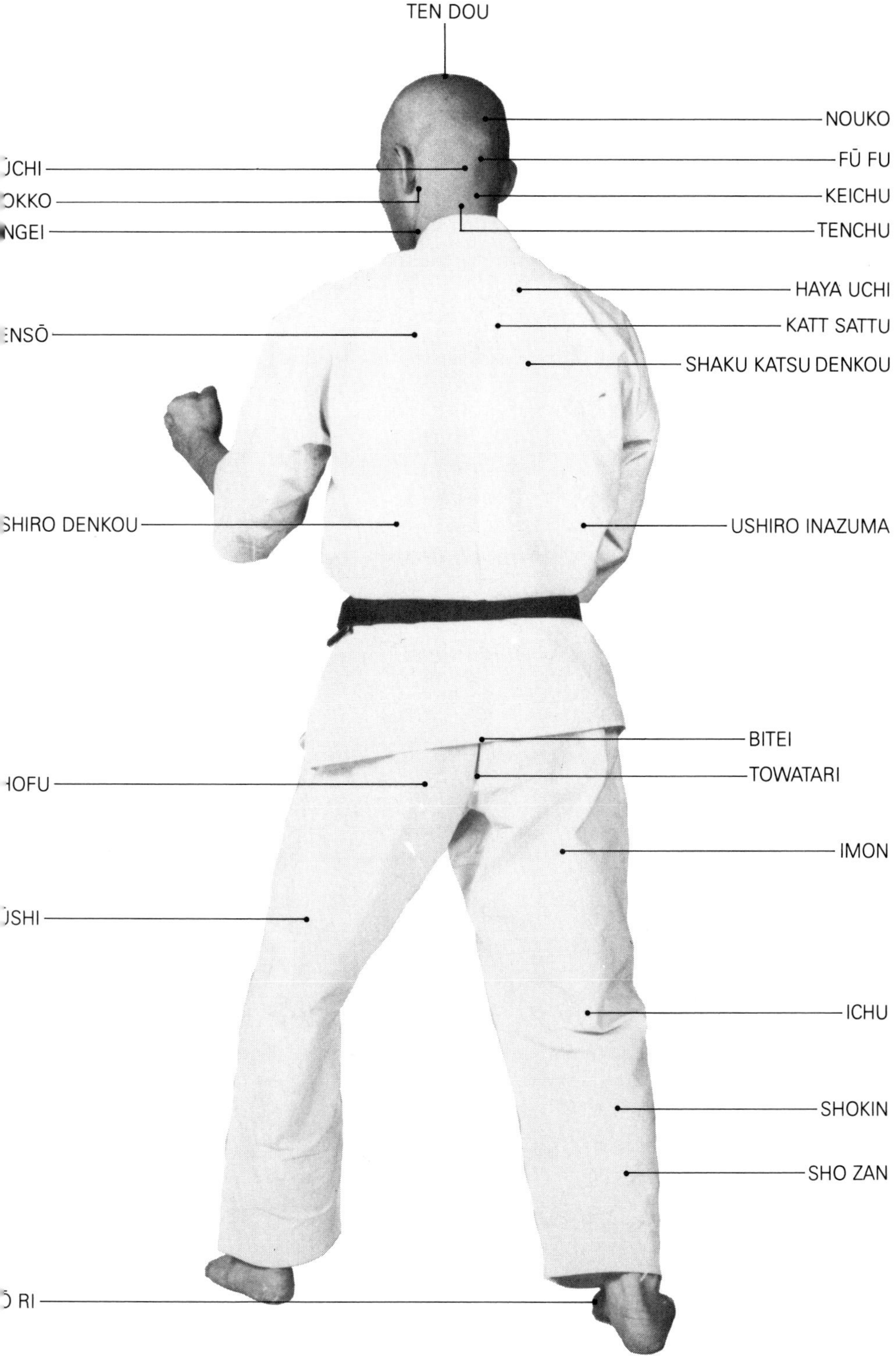

TEN DOU

NOUKO

FŪ FU

UCHI

KEICHU

OKKO

TENCHU

NGEI

HAYA UCHI

KATT SATTU

NSŌ

SHAKU KATSU DENKOU

SHIRO DENKOU

USHIRO INAZUMA

BITEI

TOWATARI

HOFU

IMON

USHI

ICHU

SHOKIN

SHO ZAN

RI

47

Control and Posture

When you first start to learn kicking techniques, you will find it very difficult to develop good posture and control because of the complexity of the movements, and the need to keep your balance when performing them. To overcome this problem in the early stages of your training, and develop really good posture and technique, practice kicking while lying on the floor as much as possible.

1. Lying on the floor...

Mawashi-Geri
Roundhouse Kick

Practice Mawashi-Geri while lying on the left and right sides, using both the ball of the foot and the instep.

2. ...hold the knee up in position prior to kicking with the ball of the foot.

3. This will enable beginners to develop the ability to keep the instep straight while the toes are bent upward.

Sokuto
Side Kick

Lying on the floor, hold the foot in position
ready to kick...

Yoko Tobi-Geri
Flying Side Kick

To practice this difficult technique, lie on
the floor and kick strongly to the side,
remembering to bring your other foot up at
the same time to protect the groin.

...exerting full power against the restraining hand...

...suddenly release the leg and kick strongly, concentrating power into the heel so that the edge of the foot turns towards the opponent and forms the 'weapon'.

A successful kick depends entirely on the correct positioning of the knee of the kicking leg, prior to the delivery of the kick. It is essential therefore that you practice this to perfection, as it is the basis of accurate and powerful kicking techniques.

When I think of training for kicking, and particularly Mae-Geri, I remember the summer training camp that I attended during my first year at university. The training was as brutally hard as the surroundings were spartan, with the day starting for us first year students when we woke up at 4a.m., to begin preparing things for the more senior students, before rousing them for the early morning exercise period, which consisted of physical jerks, long runs, and occasionally sumo training for strengthening the hips and back.

Between seven and eight, the first year students, being the most junior of the group, would be called upon to perform all the menial tasks from cooking to cleaning, and generally looking after the needs of the more senior students until at 8a.m., breakfast began. Waiting in the traditional 'seiza' position, kneeling with the legs tucked under, insteps flat on the floor and seat resting in the hollow formed by the heels, the students waited in their peer groups for grace to be said by the most senior instructor, in which we all gave thanks for the food before us, our good health and existence in the universe.

The grace finished, we began to eat. The most senior instructor gave permission for his immediate inferiors to relax and sit in a more comfortable position. They in turn passed the order onto their inferiors, and so from group to group, high to low, students relaxed, and flexing their aching limbs began to enjoy the breakfast. However, frequently the order to relax did not reach the first year students, and so we sat in agony throughout the meal, hardly aware sometimes of what we were eating because of the pain in our legs. After what seemed to us an eternity, when every instructor had put down his bowl and chopsticks and the closing grace was said, we finally rose to clear up the breakfast things, the pain coursing through our legs afresh as the circulation of blood was slowly restored to them.

At last our second batch of domestic duties were finished, and training in earnest began at 9.30. Throughout the morning we practised basic techniques, kicking and punching until we were completely exhausted. Time seemed to stand still until eventually, when all students felt that they could go on no longer, our torment was interrupted by the call to lunch at about 12.30. After a two hour break the afternoon training session began once again with basic techniques, followed by the study of pre-arranged and then free sparring, until we were finally dismissed at approximately 6.30.

Dinner at seven o'clock gave way to a seminar from eight until ten, at which all the first year students, with the exception of the lucky ones who were chosen to wait on, and attend to the needs of the senior students, once again were made to sit in 'seiza' on the hard wooden floor. Anyone who has not experienced this would find it hard to imagine the pain and discomfort it causes. Although we were already grown men, steeped in the traditions and feudal culture of our homeland, not a few eyes ran with silent tears as a result of the pain. But the tears did not help, we learnt to endure and realised in later years that our real training in Karate began here, and that we eventually became better students, and people as a result.

This was a typical day at summer training camp. When you woke up next morning, your body wracked with pain, you could hardly get out of bed, let alone stand up. The training pushed every student to his limit and beyond; there was no escape so we somehow managed through will power, reinforced by fear of failure, to get through each day until eventually, we pulled the covers over ourselves, closed our eyes and gratefully fell into the black velvet pit of the sleep of the just.

After about three days of this I was completely exhausted, when during the afternoon session, one of the instructors told me to do kicking on the spot for one hour, using the same leg. In the beginning it just seemed like hard practice, but towards the end of the hour I thought that I was going to pass out. I gave up counting how many kicks I had done, and could think only of easing my pain and tiredness by relaxing a little. I had practically no energy left, but if I slackened my efforts at all and put anything less than my total remaining power into every kick, the instructors would beat me with a bamboo practice sword to make me concentrate on performing every technique with as much strength as I could muster. Not once during this hour was I allowed to put my kicking leg down. The memory of this ordeal remains with me to this day.

We all regarded our instructors as sadistic monsters who existed only to exploit us first year students, and expose our weaknesses of technique and spirit. I asked myself time and time again as I stood on the same spot performing kick after kick why I was forced to do this. With the benefit of hindsight however, I realise just how valuable this training was to me, my instructors made me see that with good character, physical fitness and a strong spirit, there is almost no limit to what a person can achieve. They gave me knowledge, endurance and confidence, and for that I shall be eternally grateful.

I know now that what they did was for our own good. They had been through it themselves, and knew better that we did the effort and concentration of mind that was necessary to excel in the exacting art of Karate-Do.

To any new student of Karate-Do I would say that there is no easy way; if you want to succeed, the necessary pre-requisites are a good instructor, dedication, and a burning desire to improve. Fortunately, as you improve you begin to enjoy training more, as your strength and confidence grows you are spurred onto greater efforts, and if you are able to overcome the hurdles of laziness, conceit and self satisfaction, the mastery of Karate-Do will be yours.

Mae-Geri front kick is favoured by many competition fighters because of the speed with which it can be performed, and the diverse targets that it can be used to attack, ranging from the shin to the face. In fact, so popular has it become that it ranks equal favourite with the Gyaku-zuki reverse punch, the all time favourite, tournament points scorer.

As with any kicking technique, the success or failure of Mae-Geri lies in the positioning and 'snap' of the knee. While it is true that the power behind the kick is mainly generated by the hips, and the supporting leg provides the firm platform from which the kick is 'launched', it is the correct positioning of the knee that delivers the kick on target, and the snapping action that transmits the power.

As you obviously cannot practice on people to check that your kicks are effective, you must remember these important points when you train, otherwise even though your kicks may be masterpieces of balletic virtuosity, unless the knee guides and delivers the power to the target, they will lack accuracy, focus and destructive power.

Analysis of Mae-Geri

To analize Mae-Geri it is convenient to separate it into three parts, even though of course it is performed as one smooth movement. First the knee is raised into position, or as some people prefer it 'cocked' like the hammer of a gun.

Variation of Mae-Geri

This variation of Mae-Geri is frequently seen in competition, and depends upon the weight of the body being thrown forward as you kick to knock the opponent over. While visually dramatic, and impressive because of the noise that it generates, it is not really very effective and should be used only in contests.

en with the knee snapping out like a
pring being suddenly released, the whole
ower of the body is channelled through
e kicking leg, and focused into the
rget.

Finally, the leg is quickly withdrawn by
'snapping' it back and dropping it quickly to
the floor to prevent your opponent from
grabbing it.

A kick to your opponent's shin is effective in that the pain caused distracts him, and should give you a chance to push home your attack. However, to make sure that it is painful to him alone, kick the fleshiest part of his shin, not the bone.

Providing you have the speed and balance, the mid-level also becomes a target for Mae-Geri.

Kicking the knee is an excellent move, as it will at least distract your opponent allowing you an opening, or at best allow you to sweep his legs from under him.

The ribs are an available target, but they break easily so great care must be exercised, both in training and competition.

he lower abdomen is an obvious target for
e straight front kick.

These attacks to the skin, knee, groin and
lower abdominal area, are useful techniques
for smaller persons as they can compensate
for short reach, and are also extremely
effective for self defence, having a high
power/effect ratio. (Little power required to
cause great pain.)

he highest normal target for the front kick, is
he point of the chin, using the ball of the foot.

Practise Mae-Geri with the heel.

Practise kicking different targets on the body with a partner, using the heel, toes and ball of the foot.

Important

Usually, when kicking below the waist level to the shin or groin, it is often forgotten that you must not look at the area you are aiming for, as your opponent will realise what you are about to do. You should instead train yourself to look at your opponent's face while 'taking in' the rest of the space he occupies.

Tameshiwari –
Testing the Power of
Your Technique

Breaking wood will not only confirm your
skill and power, but also teach you correct
distance and 'focus', as well as toughening
your feet. But remember, unless the ball of
the foot is used correctly to strike the
wood, there is a danger of breaking some
toes, so take care to form your foot
properly. Kicking a straw makiwara
repeatedly, is also good practice for
strengthening the feet and improving
'focus'.

The Author using Mawashi-Geri roundhouse
kick to break wood at the former London
headquarters of the Wado Kai in 1965.

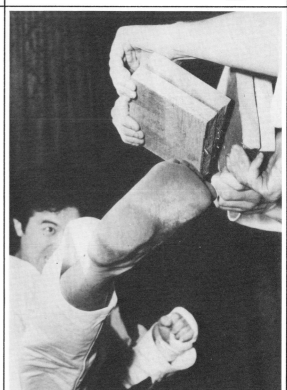

Variation of Mae-Geri & their Applications.

Mae-Geri is not as many people believe, just a straight kick to the mid-level stomach area using the ball of the foot, although I agree this is the most common variation seen. Any target, shin, knee, groin, stomach, chest and face, can be attacked with Mae-Geri, using the toes, ball of the foot, instep or heel as the striking surface.

You must practice all of these combinations and feel comfortable performing them, and also be able to deliver any variation to the target almost automatically so you do not alert your opponent by breaking your rhythm or moving unnaturally. You must be especially careful when attacking a low target, not to look down at it, as is the natural inclination of us all; rather look directly at your opponent, or through him, but never at that part of his body that you are planning to kick.

Delivering the Kick

When you are confident that you can perform strong powerful kicks that find their target, the time has come for you to master positioning, by learning to slide o jump in a half or full step as you deliver a kick, so that you effectively control the fighting distance and thereby put you adversary at a disadvantage (figs 1 & 2).

Sliding or stepping in to put yourself in the best position for you to attack from, if done smoothly and rapidly so as not to warn your opponent, can compensate for lack o height or reach on your part. Obviously your target is not going to stand still while you kick him, or even within kicking distance, so it is important that you master this closing movement, so as to effectively deliver your kicks on target, and with fu power.

For competition, mastery of the 'slide and kick' technique is essential if you want to succeed, so practice until you can do it on both sides almost without thinking, and so quickly that your opponent will have no time to react before your kick reaches him

Fig. 1.

Fig. 2.

Shin Kick. Your opponent moving his weight forward warns you of his attack to your face, which you block, simultaneously kicking him in the shin. So effective is this technique that I once saw a competitor faint after being kicked in this manner.

Similarly, in this block and Mae-Geri counter front kick, do not forget to protect your face, timing is important.

This technique is rarely used these days, and would not find favour with modern competition judges. However, in a 'do unto others before they can do it to you' type of situation, its effectiveness is such that all but the most aggressive opponent would be subdued.

To execute this movement, sweep your opponent's leg to turn his back to you...

Groin Kick. An excellent response to a lunge or reverse punch, is to block the attacking arm, and counter with a kick to the groin, using the instep as the contact area. Needless to say, it should not be necessary to use full power for this technique to be fully effective.

Mawashi-Geri: Counter. As your opponent attacks your head with a 'large' Mawashi-Geri roundhouse kick, evade the attacking foot, and at the same instant attack his groin with Mae-Geri, using the ball of your foot as the contact area. This counter attack is effective but requires perfect timing to succeed, repeated practice with a partner is therefore necessary.

..then quickly kick him in the posterior with your toes,

or on the extreme base of his spine with the ball of your foot.

Hand Grab. If you are grabbed by, or manage to grab your opponent, the best kick to use in order to free yourself, is usually Mae-Geri to the lower abdomen or groin. As your opponent catches hold of your hand...

...attack him instantly with a Mae-Geri front kick, simultaneously pulling on his grasping hand.

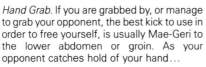

As your opponent grabs your hands...

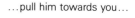

...pull him towards you...

Collar Grasp and Kick. If your opponent moves close enough to allow you to do so, grasp him by the collar...

...to pull him towards you so that you can kick him.

...and kick him, making sure that you give yourself sufficient distance and space to perform the technique properly. If you are too close, or too far away, the effect of the kick will be greatly diminished.

MAWASHI-GERI
ROUNDHOUSE
KICK

I have always considered Mawashi-Geri to be my best and favourite technique, and have tried long and hard to develop it, and hope that I shall be able to pass my experience and what skill I possess in the performance of this technique onto the reader. However, first I would like to give you some background as to how I came to choose this technique from all the kicks that exist, to be my speciality.

In my first year at University, one of my seniors called Fujimoto, a large and powerfully built man, had an exceptionally good Mawashi-Geri and won many competitions with it. I studied closely when he practised in order to learn his technique, and eventually through study and hard work, and I feel because I was well developed physically as a result of being a keen swimmer in my high school days, succeeded in developing a strong kick, that I felt was superior to those of my contemporaries.

Unfortunately, just as I was finishing my first year of University life, I suffered a bad back injury that made it necessary for me to go into hospital for prolonged treatment, that was followed by six months of out-patient care. I was in fact absent from University for a full year, and when at last I did return, my back was so weak that I could not manage a kick of any kind.

To overcome this basic weakness, I got permission from my instructor to practice only Mawashi-Geri to strengthen my back and build up my stamina, and so for many months I would perform the same number of high kicks as the other students performed low ones, developing as a result the muscles necessary for the successful performance of this demanding technique. This strenuous training made me very adept at Mawashi-Geri, and I derived much pleasure and satisfaction from its performance, and continued to train hard so as to overcome my disability and improve my technique.

Although I was training very hard and my kicks were getting stronger and stronger, I still lacked confidence even though by this time I had been awarded a brown belt. Until one day while sparring with another student, I kicked him accidentally with Mawashi-Geri and knocked him down. Although obviously regretable, and certainly unintentional on my part, this incident increased my confidence in my ability, for I knew from that day on that I could decisively defeat an opponent with a kick.

I was a brown belt for about a year, and in the second half of this period, as the dan grade examinations approached, the training was intensified. The brown belts would practise sparring with the white belts, then the other brown belts, and finally with the more experienced dan grade holders. It was hard and physically exhausting, but it did build the students to a peak, and gave them more confidence in themselves.

About this time I fought a bout with a man named Hirano, then at the peak of his ability, and considered by all to be a very fine fighter. I, on the other hand was

inexperienced, but made up for this with over confidence and strong fighting spirit, to the extent that I was arrogant enough to believe that I could beat this awesome adversary by using Mawashi-Geri. When the match began, I immediately attacked his head with my favourite technique, but his superior ability and experience allowed him to easily avoid my powerful attack and catching my leg, threw me to the ground. This humiliation, as I viewed it, taught me that fighting spirit, enthusiasm and limitless confidence are not enough to defeat a skilled and experienced fighter. Mr. Hirano, to whom I shall be forever grateful for this knowledge, moved to Hawaii to teach Karate, and later I believe went to the United States.

This experience allowed me to take my first steps along the path of Karate-Do and confirmed my desire to really excel at kicking, particularly with the roundhouse kick. The second experience that shaped my early career happened a short time later at the dan gradings held for University students from the Kanto area of Japan, at which I was awarded first dan. One of the opponents that I fought gave me a lesson that I never forgot. I was sure that I could beat him, but every time I attacked, he would precisely, and I regret to say successfully, attack my groin with a front kick that beat my defences completely. In desperation I put all my effort into a powerful jumping kick, but the result was just the same, his accurate and perfectly timed technique still found its target.

I was surprised and impressed by this, that

after the competition I asked one of my instructors, Mr. Nakano, to tell me everything he knew about kicks to the groin. Armed with this knowledge, I practised these techniques night and day, until I too could perform devastating kicks to the groin that within two years would earn me the reputation of a hard aggressive fighter that possessed two especially dangerous techniques.

Despite the advances that I made in technique, mentally I was still very immature at this time, too sure of myself, too confident for my own good in fact. The hard training that I received from instructors Hirano and Nakano, and the numerous kicks and punches they gave me, eventually brought me to my senses and made me realise that there were better, stronger and wiser people in the world than me, and that unless I put aside my over confidence and arrogance, I would not progress. Arrogance as expressed by satisfaction with one's performance and pride in it, is one of the greatest enemies of the Karate student as it leads to slackening of training with the inevitable result that improvement of technique cannot be achieved. If you do not train hard it is like a man planting a tree but failing to water it, it is not enough just to know how to perform Karate techniques, you must also practice them.

From those days to this, I have believed that you should train really hard using the whole varied range of karate techniques, but also give special attention to those that suit you as an individual best. I have personally found that by doing this an overall benefit will result.

It is important that you understand that Mawashi-Geri can be used to attack almost any part of your opponent's body.

1. To perform Mawashi-Geri raise the knee and holding it as high as possible...

2. ...suddenly snap the kicking leg forward explosively, adding the power of the hips as your leg rises towards the target.

3. Immediately the kick is completed, snap the kicking leg back so that it cannot be seized by your opponent.

ttack the inside of your opponent's thigh or
ee using the ball of the foot.

This time attack the outside of his thigh or
knee using the ball of the foot.

most effective technique is a rising kick to
e area of the groin, using the instep.

This attack to the lower abdomen can be
made with the ball of the foot or the toes.

A kick to the inside of your opponent's blocking arm can weaken his defence and lay him open to a follow up attack.

Mid-level attack to the body using the ball of the foot.

Attacking the muscle just below the elbow will cause your opponent considerable discomfort, and may open up his defence.

This attack to the back can be made with the ball of the foot or instep.

is attack to the neck with the ball of the ot is powerful and effective.

hen you feel that your training has made u competent enough to kick any target on ur opponent's body, practice with a partner / making him attack you with a punch for ample, and defend using Mawashi-Geri as counterattack.

Although requiring great control, this kick to the chin or jaw with the instep and ball of foot will usually close a contest when properly performed.

You must do this repeatedly, as fast as you can, so that your 'body' learns the movement instinctively, and you can perform it without conscious thought.

Fig. 1.   Fig. 2.

I hope you will have realised from the examples given that Mawashi-Geri is not only performed in the traditional 'large' fashion, but should be made to fit the circumstances. In this respect it is a very flexible technique, particularly for use as a counterattack, where it can be scaled down to match the attack being made on you. For example in fig 1 an attack utilising a punch can be defeated by a large classical kick, while in fig 2 the opponent's 'large' attack can be beaten using a 'small' Mawashi-Geri to his groin.

So remember, learn to match your kick to the circumstances, Mawashi-Geri is versatile and powerful technique which properly mastered, can be used with devastating effect. The opponent that will give you the opportunity to kick him with the traditional form of this technique rare, so train yourself to deliver roundhouse kicks of every type, from an position.

The photographs show Mawashi-Geri being used as a counterattack after you have caught your opponent's arm.

It is essential you keep your elbows close to your body while you exert a forwards downward pressure, (towards you) on the arm, to keep your opponent off balance.

You must make sure that you grasp his wrist from above, so that it is held tightly in the palm of your hand, which should face downwards.

Practice with a partner so that you can develop fast reactions and a sense of timing that will allow you to grasp your attacker's arm...

...and then use it to restrain and control him as you launch your counterattack. Only repeated practice using full speed and power will develop this skill.

If your opponent manages to catch your arm, kick him somewhere below the waist, so you can use a small movement that will not warn him of your intention to attack.

A kick to the knee or groin is usually effective under these circumstances.

you have to face an armed opponent, never
~y to defend yourself with your hands, but
ily on a kick so as to keep as far away from
he weapon as possible.

his variation of Mawashi-Geri, is performed
rom inside to out, that is, curving away from
our body as you kick instead of towards it in
he conventional manner.

Tell yourself that you have only the one kick to
defeat the aggressor, so you must make it
count.

It is particularly suitable for kicks to the groin
using the instep...

Training Hints

To kick effectively, you must build stror legs and hips, and develop a really goc sense of balance. You must also tra yourself to kick with both legs so that yc can use them as freely as you do yor hands. To achieve this, perform all bas kicking techniques repeatedly as part ↨ your general training, then to develop goc balance, stand on one leg and perforr double kicks, for example Mawashi-Ger Mae-Geri, Mawashi-Geri/Ushiro-Geri wit out putting the kicking leg down. The repeat this exercise on the other side ∢ the body.

...and is also very effective for kicking to the chin, as the opponent rarely sees your foot as it curves upwards from below his line of sight, and is therefore given no warning whatsoever.

This double kick or 'Ke-Kaeshi' (literally kick and return) uses the first kick to the knee or inner thigh to unsettle or unbalance the opponent and open up the groin for attacking; then another simultaneous groin

kick to beat him before he can recover h balance. The second kick must be performe immediately after the first, and without ar hesitation; the kicking foot does not touc the floor throughout the movement.

SOKUTO-GERI SIDE KICK

Sokuto is generally considered to be one of the most difficult kicks, more difficult for example than Mae-Geri or Mawashi-Geri, due to the greater involvement of the hips in its performance. If you can master this technique, you will be able to use it to great effect in competition, particularly as it is rarely seen these days in this context, and most opponents therefore, will not know how to defend themselves against it.

The 'grand master' of Sokuto must be Tatsuo Suzuki Hanshi 8th Dan, presently chief instructor to Europe, and at the time to which I refer, a senior member of the Nihon University Karate Club. His formidable reputation had been built on his ability as a strong and expert kicker who specialised in Sokuto-Geri. In fact, so fast and powerful was his performance of his 'forte' that it came to be known as 'Suzuki's Sokuto'.

In those days competition as such was unknown, so the meetings that took place between university karate teams were known as 'exchange exercise'. This was hardly an accurate description, as they were more often than not, blood baths, with both sides doing their utmost to win, and at the same time study and learn the techniques of their opponents, so that defensive techniques could be developed to counter them.

In his third year of university life, Suzuki Sensei attended just such an 'exchange' that was held annually between our own university in Tokyo, and another well known educational institution in the Kansei area of western Japan. 'Suzuki's Sokuto' beat every student in the Dojo which was a great honour for us, and a severe humiliation for our opponents. I noticed that when Suzuki Sensei's kick made contact with his opponent, the power of the technique caused the unlucky victim to jacknife forward from the waist. I had always thought that, as with most other kicks, when contact was squarely made, the recipient would be thrown away by the force. But in the case of 'Suzuki's Sokuto' they bent in the middle like a cooked shrimp.

The following year he returned to this same event hoping to repeat his performance of the previous meeting. Contrary to his expectations however, he failed to win a single contest with his favourite technique, and ended the event a perplexed and worried man. After the event we met the opposing team, and so anxious was Suzuki Sensei because of his poor performance, that he asked their chief instructor for his opinion in the hope that he might find the solution to his problem.

To our great surprise, he replied that due to the humiliation inflicted by Suzuki Sensei on his team the previous year, his students had concentrated all their efforts on developing defences against Sokuto-Geri for the past twelve months, to avoid a similar humiliation at this event. I think this illustrates very well how in those days, karate students were willing to spend a year, or two even, mastering a particular technique, polishing it to perfection and making it their own.

In this day and age, Karate is being made into a modern sport, and the techniques are being simplified year by year so that students of average and low ability are able to perform them in competition. Regretably, as a result of this, all the difficult and effective but potentially dangerous techniques are becoming extinct. This is true of every country in the world where Karate is practised, and while I welcome with some reservations, the emergence of a modern form of Karate-Do as an international sport, I also feel that it would be a tragedy if these powerful techniques, that are so effective for self-defence, and that have been passed down from generation to generation, should be lost to the generations that will follow.

s Sokuto-Geri is a difficult technique, it must be learnt thoroughly from beginning to end in
tages so that eventually, you can perform it fluently, powerfully and with good 'form'. Start off
y practising turning the outside edge of the foot forward to form a cutting edge (Sokuto
ctually means leg-sword) with the leg held in the preparatory position.
hen execute a smooth downward stamping motion, keeping the foot positioned as shown.
hrust the leg forward when you kick, making sure the edge of the foot stays pointed towards
our target by applying power to your heel. Practice kicking to different targets.

When, through practice, you have acquired
power and accuracy, add the thrust of the
hips to the technique to give it maximum
effect. Practice kicking to all levels as if you
were attacking an opponent's legs, body or
head. Repeated practice is essential for
mastery of this technique.

Kicking Combinations

When you feel that you have mastered
Sokuto, practice it in combination with
other kicking techniques, such as Mae-
Geri, by performing one kick, then
snapping the leg back and immediately
performing another without putting the
kicking leg down. This exercise will teach
you the correct movement of the hips
required to kick successfully, and also
develop the perfect balance that is so
essential. Practice as many combinations
of kicks as you can think of, their number is
limited only by your imagination.

Focusing the Kick

1. When you perform Sokuto-Geri, you must
'focus' the kick correctly so that it has
maximum effect on the target. If you are
attacking your opponent's knee, don't look
down and warn him of your intention,
otherwise he will automatically move his leg
back, changing the fighting distance, and
ruining your focus.

Sokuto-Geri attack to the body.

3. High level Sokuto attack.

Attacking the Knee

This classic and most effective attack, is performed by stamping down at the inside or outside of your opponent's knee.

1. Normal fighting stance.

Throat/Chin Attack

1. Standing at normal fighting distance...

2. ...quickly slide your backleg in half a step to put you at your preferred fighting distance...

Prepare to kick by raising the knee and shing the front 'edge' forward.

3. Stamp down hard to your opponent's knee.

...then raising the leg and 'cocking' the ee ready to kick...

4. ...stamp the front edge of your foot into your opponent's throat or chin.

To increase the power of the kick, and extend its range, use the 'snap' of the hips to help deliver the technique. The sliding half-step and kick which precedes this must be simultaneous.

1. Normal fighting stance and distance.

1. Practice lifting the knee high…

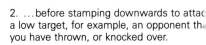

2. …before stamping downwards to attac a low target, for example, an opponent th you have thrown, or knocked over.

A simultaneous sliding half-step and
ck...

3. ...uses the twisting movement or 'snap'
of the hips, to drive home to the target.

3. Example of low level attack on an
opponent who is lying on the floor.

The ability to perform effective combination techniques is a valuable one, and the only way that this skill will be acquired is by constantly practising the sort of drills that follow, with an opponent.

1. Attack your opponent's blocking arm wi Mikazuki-Geri, crescent kick...

Practice using Sokuto-Geri to stop a frontal attack. This requires much practice.

Use the extra distance that thrusting forwa with the hips gives you, to out-distance yo opponent, and block his attack.

2. ...then snapping the leg back...

3. ...kick him again using Sokuto-Geri in one movement.

Avoid your opponent's powerful Mawashi-Geri roundhouse kick, and sliding quickly in, kick his supporting leg strongly.

Forestall your opponent's front kick attack, by kicking his shin with Sokuto. Practice using Sokuto-Geri against as many punches and kicks as possible.

1. Grab your opponent, and pulling him towards you to break his balance...

As a general rule, when attacking the knee or hip joint of an opponent, pull his arm upward, and when attacking the armpit, pull it downwards.

1. Having caught your opponent's arm, 'cock' your leg ready to kick and either...

...kick him in the back of the knee to bring   3. Or (as shown from the other side) kick his
n down.   neck with Sokuto.

...drive your foot into his hip joint...   3. ...or his armpit.

Kicking techniques provide a good defence against an armed assailant because of the extra distance they give you. Needless to say, any armed person is dangerous, so practice these techniques thoroughly before you have to call upon them for defence of your person.

1. After your opponent seizes your wrist, grab <u>his</u> wrist, and pulling him towards you...

1. Dropping low to avoid the knife attack, kick the assailant in the stomach or armpit.

...kick him once, then pulling your leg quickly back...

3. ...attack the knee of his rear leg with Sokuto.

Avoiding the knife thrust, attack the assailant's knee with Sokuto-Geri.

Sokuto-Geri gives the distinct advantage of extra reach to the performer, as the leg is fully extended when kicking, and the upper part of the body leans back slightly, away from the opponent. This makes it particularly useful for small people, or those fighting an opponent with a very long reach.

I have fought some people who were expert with a Sokuto-Geri, and it is a very difficult kick to beat if it is performed properly. But remember, as with all kicking techniques, it must be practised until it is perfect, so that you can use it almost without thinking, and certainly without giving your opponent any warning.

USHIRO-GERI BACK KICK

Introduction

When I was a student I saw the then instructor of Nihon University Karate Club, Fumihiro Tanabe, conclusively beat an opponent using Ura Mawashi-Geri, reverse roundhouse kick, and was greatly inspired by his performance. First he drove his opponent into a corner, then, turning round very quickly, he attacked so fast with Ura Mawashi-Geri to the unfortunate's chin that the latter hit the floor without ever realising what had happened.

It was interesting to see how, at the instant that Tanabe Sensei turned his back, his opponent quite naturally, and instinctively sensing that the danger from his attacker had lessened, relaxed slightly, never thinking for an instant that a split second later his antagonist's heel would hit him on the chin knocking him senseless. However, the very fact that to perform these powerful heel kicks to the rear, Ura Mawashi-Geri and Ushiro-Geri, requires you to turn your back on your opponent, limits their use to opponents of equal or preferably inferior skill and experience.

Do not use these techniques indiscriminately in competition, as they require much hard training to perfect, and if performed badly against an experienced opponent, will make you vulnerable to a counter-attack. However, as shown by Tanabe Sensei, if they are used intelligently, against the right sort of opponent they can be devastatingly effective, the key to success is to know your opponent and yourself, if on balance you feel that you are superior in skill and experience, your chances of success are good.

From your basic fighting stance...

2. ...move your leading leg around and turn 180°.

Then raising the knee, snap the leg out at ▮e target, turning your ankle so as to kick ▮ith the heel...

4. ...then quickly draw your leg back, staying alert to your opponent's reactions at all time. When performing kicks to the rear it is important that you look into your opponent's eyes so that you can monitor his reactions. This however can result in lack of accuracy and focus, compared with looking at his whole body as is usually the case, and must therefore be compensated for, or the kick will not be fully effective.

Application 1
Mikazuki/Ushiro-Geri
Combination

Most kicks to the rear are performed by turning around completely and then kicking, a variation of this is to combine the kick with a frontal attack which breaks the opponent's balance, so that you can take advantage of the weak moment created to kick him. For example Mikazuki-Geri to your opponent's arm as shown, followed by Ushiro-Geri. Needless to say, because of the speed, timing and balance required, much practice is necessary to master this sort of combination.

It is essential that when you resume your normal fighting stance, you pay great attention to your opponent, you must not relax even if the kick has reached its target successfully, but must remain constantly alert. Kicking directly to the rear is very difficult, even though it may not seem so to the casual observer.

Application 2
Ushiro Kakato-Geri
Groin Kick

Move into attacking distance by sliding your back leg behind the leading one, (this movement also helps to give the necessary 'twist' to your body). Then launch your attack from a balanced position on the back leg. In the case of a kick to the groin as shown in this example, the leg rises as the attack is made until it makes contact. The secret of performing any kick of this sort is to move the back leg in as quickly and smoothly as possible as you prepare to kick, so that you give your opponent no warning of your forthcoming attack.

These 2 examples show attacks being made to the mid and upper levels using Ushiro-Geri. Always remember to return to your original fighting stance as soon as possible after completing the kick, and stay alert at all times, and especially after you have completed an attack.

Application 3
Escape from Hold Applied from the Rear

When grasped from behind by an assailant, move around as if trying break his hold, then, while he is distracted and you have given yourse the right distance, kick him in the groin with your heel. As a general ru when you are seized from behind, keep moving continually to preve your antagonist consolidating his hold, and to give yourself time to fi the weakness that will allow you to break away. If you have an arm or l free, keep punching and kicking until he decides that it is wisest to l you go.

URA MAWASHI-GERI
REVERSE ROUNDHOUSE KICK

This kick, which as the name applies is a reversed form of the roundhouse kick, is difficult to control, and must therefore be used wisely. When you spin round to perform this kick, the large swinging motion has the tendency to unbalance you, so great care must be used to prevent this. A difficult technique to use against an opponent who is your equal in skill and determination.

Ura Mawashi-Geri
Reverse Roundhouse Kick

Application 1
Step in and Kick to the Leg

As you glide in with your rear leg, block your opponent's hands to distract him and prevent an attack, then kick the outside, or rear of his leg with Ura Mawashi-Geri, using a 'hooking' motion.

Application 2
Kicks to the Back and Head

As with application 1 slide in with the rear foot and kick to the back or the head with strong 'hooking' motion.

pplication 3
tacks from the Inside

Attack your opponent at any level by sliding in and attacking from the 'inside' using a 'hooking' action to deliver the kick with the heel.

Application 4

Sweep your opponent's leading leg, the
while he is unbalanced, attack his fac
with Ura Mawashi-Geri.

KAKATO-GERI
HEEL KICK

Introduction

This kick, which is the one most commonly known by the term 'Kakato-Geri' or heel kick, is an extremely effective one, in fact dangerously so, and notoriously difficult to control, which has led it to be banned from competition by many Karate organisations.

It is performed by swinging the leg as high as possible, then pulling it sharply downwards onto your opponent's head or body.

Important Points

Practice each kicking technique, (and any other technique for that matter) until you can perform it almost without thinking. Study timing so that you can not only react more quickly at any given time, but at precisely the right time, and above all else, when you perform a technique commit yourself to it totally. Do not waiver, or change your mind, perform the technique to the best of your ability using your full power and concentration, then move smoothly onto the next and perform it in the same manner.

Watch your opponent carefully at all times, but avoid concentrating your gaze on one part of his body; rather, look at him as a whole from head to toe, so that you are aware of the slightest movement he makes.

Keep moving and you will be able to take advantage of any opening your opponent gives you, as well as defending yourself effectively.

However strong your kicks and punches are, if you blink when your opponent attacks you, he will have enough time to complete his attack. Even if your skills are very good, and your reaction time low, one blink, that split second when the brain is robbed of visual stimuli, may result in your defeat.

Therefore you must train yourself not to blink in response to an attacker's feigned or real attack, but attack him the instant that you sense he is about to attack you.

Application 1 Kick to Chest
Swing your leg up, either directly in front you, inside or outside...

Application 3
Against an Attack from the Rear
If you are grasped from behind...

.then drive it downwards with as much force as possible to strike your opponent's head, shoulder, chest or thigh with your heel.

Application 2 Strike to Instep

This useful and effective self defence technique is performed by raising your leg and stamping your heel hard into your opponent's instep.

.stamping down on your attacker's instep sing your heel...

...will quickly persuade him to release his grip.

Application 4
To Release a Hold

To break free of an opponent's hold, swing your leg up and drive it down into his elbow to force him to the floor.

Hiza-Geri is a powerful technique that is usually performed by grabbing your opponent at the moment you clash, then pulling him towards you so you can kick him with your knee.

A variation of this that I sometimes used when I was a student, involves throwing your opponent to the floor, then as you feign a punch to the area of his face, you actually attack his abdomen by falling and thrusting your knee into it. Needless to say this is an extremely dangerous move that must only be practised with great caution, and should only truly be used in a life threatening situation. Another variation is Tobi Hiza-Geri, or jumping knee kick, in which you leap forward at your opponent as you attack him with your knee.

Each variation of this powerful technique should be practised, as they can all be used effectively when a suitable situation arises.

...as you close with your opponent, grab him by the neck (or ears, hair or collar) and pulling him towards you...

...drive your knee into his groin or stomach using the entire power of your body.

As with the previous technique, grab your opponent, and swinging your knee up and around, strike him in the side or chest...

...or by pulling him further forward, the head.

If your opponent has succeeded in grabbing both your wrists, feign an escape attempt, and as he reacts by tensing himself...

...use his energy to pull him towards you ar kick him.

Having thrown your opponent to the floor, keep hold of him so you can control his movement, and prevent him rolling away from you. Distract him by feigning a blow to his face...

...then drive your knee into his stomac (See cautionary notice in the introduction t this chapter.)

This is an effective block that can be used against Mae-Geri front kick, or Mawashi-Geri roundhouse kick, and is especially useful as it permits immediate retaliation.

As your opponent attacks, raise your knee to intercept his kick, taking care to keep your weight forward so that you can immediately counterattack while he is off balance. The blocking leg must be dropped down to the floor as soon as possible, so that your opponent cannot 'sweep' your supporting leg.

MIKAZUKI-GERI CRESCENT KICK

This technique takes its name from the similarity of the curved path the foot describes when performing it, to the shape of the crescent, or literally 'one third moon'. Hence: Mikazuki = crescent moon, Geri = kick.

As this technique alone is not usually powerful enough to finish a strong opponent, it is used mainly as one of a series, or combination of techniques, in which the role it fulfils is in breaking the opponent's balance in order to make him vulnerable to the techniques that follow. While the target for this kick can be virtually anywhere on the body, it is most often used against the opponent's leading leg, using the sole of the foot as the contact area, to break his balance and knock him down.

Mikazuki-Geri is not a technique that should be studied in isolation, for as I have already said, it lacks the power to finish a contest. However, when used as the initial move in a fast and smoothly executed combination of techniques, it can become the platform from which an overwhelming attack can be launched. By 'fast and smoothly executed' I mean techniques that are performed with such speed, power and continuity, that there is no apparent gap between them that would allow an opponent to defend himself or counterattack.

In the instant that your opponent warns you of his intention to attack by lunging forward and attempting to strike your face, block the attacking arm with your hand and at the same time, kick his leading leg with Mikazuki-Geri using a strong 'sweeping' motion, with the sole of the foot striking your opponent's leg. If correctly timed and executed, this is usually enough to knock down the strongest fighter, and leave him extremely vulnerable to your <u>immediate</u> follow up.

In the case of an armed assailant, use Mikazuki-Geri against the attacking arm, then follow through immediately with any technique that suits the circumstances, and that will render the attacker harmless in the shortest possible time, with the least chance of injury to yourself.

SUTEMI WAZA
SACRIFICE
TECHNIQUES

Tobi-Geri	Flying Front Kick
Yoko Tobi-Geri	Flying Side Kick
Tobi Mawashi-Geri	Flying Roundhouse Kick
Nidan-Geri	Flying Double Kick
Tobi Ushiro Mawashi-Geri	Flying Reverse Roundhouse Kick

Flying kicks are not separate Karate movements, but basic kicking techniques to which a jump, off what would normally be the supporting leg, is added. They are essentially the same basic kicking techniques that you studied when you first started Karate, with minor variations of performance incorporated to compensate for any increased vulnerability (e.g. in Yoko Tobi Geri, the non kicking leg is drawn up to protect the groin) caused by being airborne.

When you perform these, for what I have described for want of a better word as 'sacrifice techniques' both of your feet are obviously off the floor, so when you land you may lose your balance for an instant and be unprepared to continue the attack or defend yourself. This will give your opponent a perfect opportunity to attack you in your moment of weakness, and so you must learn to continue your attack while airborne if your kick fails, so that you can avoid this moment of complete vulnerability. If you can achieve this, your opponent, who will be waiting for you when you land, will be caught unawares, and you can still beat him.

If you fail to do this you will suffer the fate of a student that I saw fight a senior instructor

called Fujii, in my student days. The flying attack was made, but Fujii Sensei, remaining completely calm and composed as a result of his experience and skill, easily avoided the onslaught, and mercilessly attacked his opponent at the precise moment he landed, knocking him to the ground.

For this reason it is extremely unwise to attempt these techniques on persons who are your superiors in skill and experience, or when fighting more than one opponent. Although they are extremely attractive to watch, and breathtakingly dynamic when captured on film, they are in fact almost impossible to perform successfully in competition. These days, partly I think because of the influence of martial arts films, I see many students attempting to win competitions with Tobi Mawashi-Geri, (flying roundhouse kick) and Tobi Ushiro Mawashi-Geri, (flying reverse roundhouse kick), and although I agree that these techniques should be studied, and studied intensively, I feel that because they are of limited practical value, they should not be given priority over the more basic skills, which you will find much more useful for winning competitions or defending yourself.

So when should these 'Sutemi Waza' techniques be used? Let me counsel you like this.

If you have attacked your opponent with all the techniques you know, and all have failed and defeat looks inevitable, then attack with a flying kick. Choose your moment wisely, and when he least expects it, launch your attack as strongly as possible in the hope that this sudden onslaught will unbalance him, and give you the match.

At the instant before you attack, your mind must be completely clear and free of concern. If you can achieve this state, then your chances of success are greatly enhanced. To understand the meaning of this, please consider this old saying, much used by exponents of traditional Japanese Fencing.

Kiri musubu yaiba no shita koso jigoku nare
Fumikomi ikeba sokoga gokuraku.

Roughly translated, this means that beneath the blade of your opponent's sword lies hell; One step further heaven can be found: The message is that even when your enemy has his sword raised ready to strike you down, one final mighty effort with a clear state of mind, one last step forward to close with him can give you the result you seek, and allow you to snatch victory from the jaws of death.

A saying attributed to Hakuin Zenshi explains this concept of 'mu' or nothingness as follows:–

Wakaishuya shinunoga iyanara ima shiniyare
Hitotabi shineba mou shinanu.

This means that if you fear dying, consider yourself to be already dead: as you are now dead, you cannot die a second time. We must understand from this that before we make that last attack on the enemy, we must completely empty our minds, and believe ourselves to be dead. In this state of 'mu' doubt, fear or desire to win do not exist and we are free to act instinctively and without emotion. It is this state that followers of Zen Buddhism seek to achieve when they meditate.

Practice attacking from varying distances and do not under any circumstances warn your opponent of your intentions by dropping your hips, or adopting a particular stance prior to attacking. Teach yourself to jump and kick from any position so as to achieve complete surprise, and therefore, maximum effect.

Tetsu Geta, or iron clogs of the tradition Japanese type, are a useful training a that, if used correctly, will rapidly bui muscle and improve kicking power an technique. Choose a pair that a reasonably comfortable, and not too heav otherwise they will tend to come undor too easily.

Before training with tetsu geta, it essential that you warm up thoroughly b performing stretching exercises so as avoid strains and sprains that are cause when cold muscles are worked too har After you finish training with the clog continue practising kicks, and then finall do a complete set of stretching exercise again, to relax the muscles of the legs an hips. Make sure that you secure the clog tightly to your feet in the manner show in this chapter, so that they do not com loose and fly off to injury somebody. you feel the binding coming loose, sto immediately and re-tie them.

Remember that, being made of cast iro the clogs tend to be very slippery on som surfaces, therefore great care must b exercised when using them. When I was student we would often go jogging, or ru up and down stairs in tetsu geta, and I ofte found it difficult to keep my balance However they are an extremely valuab training aid, which, when used correctl will certainly prove beneficial.

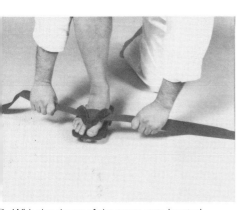

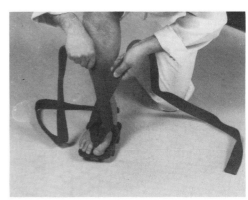

1. With the thong of the tetsu geta located between the large and second toes, pass a karate belt under the sole of the clogs, between the two iron blocks.

2. Bring the ends of the belt up and cross them over your instep.

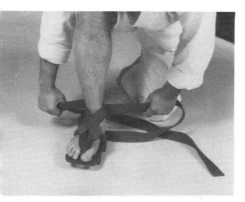

3. Pull the belt tight then pass both ends around the back of your ankle and return them to the front.

4. Cross the ends of the belt over once more and...

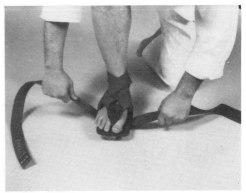

5. ...pull them tight.

6. Pass the ends under the clogs and between the blocks for a second time...

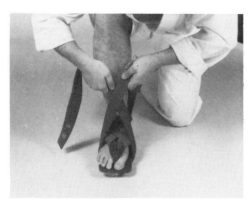

7. ...pull the ends up towards you, and crossing them over...

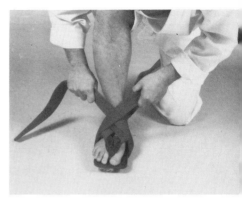

8. ...pass them behind the ankle...

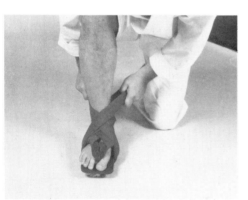

9. ...and returning them to the front...

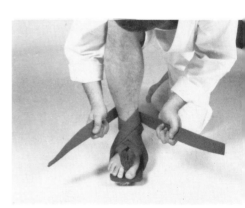

10. ...pull them tight.

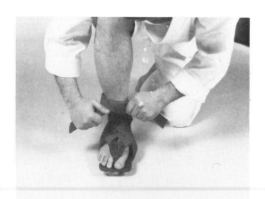

11. Tie the ends securely in a knot in front of the ankle.

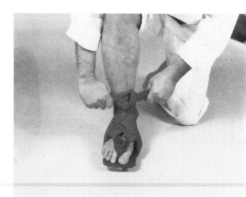

12. Iron clog shown correctly tied to the foot, secure the other in exactly the same fashion.

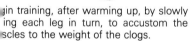

in training, after warming up, by slowly
ing each leg in turn, to accustom the
scles to the weight of the clogs.

When you are fully warmed up, you can start
to perform kicks at full power while wearing
the iron geta.

ctice all the techniques, Sokuto,
washi-Geri etc.

Each kicking technique places emphasis on
different sets of muscles. You must practice
all of them therefore, to maintain balanced
progress.

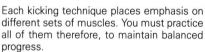

This static exercise will develop strong abdominal muscles.

CAUTION

To prevent strains and pulled muscles, 'warm up' before using tetsu-geta, and 'warm down' afterwards. Junior students should not train with tetsu-geta until they have stopped growing.

Kiri musubu yaiba no shita koso jigoku nare
Fumikomi ikeba sokoga gokuraku

Wakaishuya shinunoga iyanara ima shiniyare
Hitotabi shineba mou shinanu.

From Budō Houkan

Nunchaku Dynamic Training
By Hirokazu Kanazawa 8th Dan **$10.95**

Dynamic Power of Karate
By Hirokazu Kanazawa 8th Dan **$15.95**

Shotokan Advanced Kata Series
By Keinosuke Enoeda **$15.95** *per volume*

Volume 1
Bassai-Dai : Kanku-Dai : Jion : Empi : Hangetsu

Volume 2
Bassai-sho : Kanku-sho : Jiin : Gankaku : Sochin

Volume 3
Tekki-Nidan : Tekki-Sandan *(2 versions)* : Nijushiho
: Gojushiho-Dai : Gojushiho-sho

Volume 4
Jitte : Chinte : Unsu : Meikyo (Rohai)
: Wankan *(in preparation)*

Shadow of the Ninja
By Katsumi Toda **$8.95**

Revenge of the Shogun's Ninja
By Katsumi Toda **$8.95**

Ninja Death Vow
By Katsumi Toda **$8.95**

The Ninja Star – Art of Shuriken Jutsu
By Katsumi Toda **$7.95**

Ninja Training Manual
By Yukishiro Sanada **$10.95**

Balisong – Iron Butterfly
By C. Hernandez **$8.95**

Close Encounters
By Takayuki Kubota 8th Dan **$12.95**

Kubotan Keychain – Instrument of Attitude Adjustment
By Takayuki Kubota 8th Dan **$8.95**

Naked Blade
By Toshishiro Obata 7th Dan **$10.95**

Crimson Steel
By Toshishiro Obata 7th Dan **$10.95**

Kama – Weapon Art of Okinawa
By Toshishiro Obata 7th Dan **$10.95**

Samurai Aikijutsu
By Toshishiro Obata 7th Dan **$12.95**

Ninja Sword – Art of Silent Kenjutsu
By Katsumi Toda **$8.95**

When The Going Gets Tough
By Colonel M. Smythe **$8.95**

Please direct any enquiries regarding our publications to:

Dragon Publishing Corporation
P.O. Box 6039 Thousand Oaks
California 91359 USA